# As Birds Do

Mary MacRae

# As Birds Do

*Sirra, your Fathers dead,*
*And what will you do now? How will you live?*
*As birds do Mother.*
*What with wormes, and flyes?*
*With what I get I meane, and so do they.*

*Macbeth IV ii*

Second Light Publications

First published 2007
by Second Light Publications
9 Greendale Close
London
SE22 8TG

www.secondlightlive.co.uk



ISBN: 978-0-9546934-3-5

British Library Cataloguing-in-Publication Data
A catalogue record for this book is available from the British Library.

Cover artwork and design by Martin Parker at silbercow.co.uk

Printed by Media Services copy@mediaservices.org.uk

for Lachlan

## ACKNOWLEDGEMENTS

Some of these poems or versions of them have appeared in the following magazines and anthologies: *The Interpreter's House, London Poets, Magma, Orbis, PN Review, Quattrocento, Scintilla, Second Light Newsletter*, *Staple*, *Entering the Tapestry, a second anthology from The Poetry School* (Enitharmon, 2003), *Making Worlds* (Headland Publications, 2003), *Four Caves of the Heart* (Second Light Publications, 2004), *Images of Women* (Arrowhead Press in association with Second Light, 2006), *this little stretch of life* (Hearing Eye, 2006), the third anthology from The Poetry School, *I Am Twenty People* (Enitharmon, 2007) and in *The Forward book of poetry 2008*.

Many thanks to Mimi Khalvati for all she has taught me about poetry and for her comments and advice while I was compiling this collection.

Many thanks, too, to Myra Schneider for her close reading of my poems and for her editorial advice and support, and to Dilys Wood for her suggestions and encouragement.

Particular thanks are also due to members of The Poetry School's Advanced Poetry Workshop who provided constant stimulus and keen criticism while I was writing many of these poems.

CONTENTS


| | |
|---|---|
| The Various Light | 9 |
| Glose: Water and Stone | 10 |
| Newfoundland | 12 |
| At the Party | 13 |
| Opus 20 | 15 |
| Ritornello | 16 |
| For V.H. | 17 |
| Wild Life | 18 |
| The End of Time | 19 |
| At Laugharne | 20 |
| Reading Traherne | 21 |
| Visitants | 22 |
| Soundings | 24 |
| As Dew | 25 |
| Life Story | 26 |
| Cow Parsley | 28 |
| By Faversham Creek | 29 |
| Mewslade Bay | 30 |
| Hiraeth | 32 |
| Free Fall | 33 |
| Flycatcher | 35 |
| Sonnets for a Child | 36 |
| The Road | 40 |
| The Clearing | 41 |
| Love Song | 43 |
| The Buoy | 44 |
| Dungeness | 45 |
| Laundry | 46 |

| | |
|---|---|
| Accommodation | 48 |
| Jury | 50 |
| The Fall | 51 |
| What You Called Me | 52 |
| Grace | 53 |
| Rio Darro | 54 |
| In Granada | 55 |
| Easter Candles | 56 |
| On Oare Marshes | 60 |
| Desire | 61 |
| Lords and Ladies | 62 |
| White Cyclamen | 63 |
| Towards the Deep North | 64 |
| Morandi's Jugs | 65 |
| Blue Tits | 66 |
| Gannet | 67 |

## THE VARIOUS LIGHT

On the afternoon of the day he died she looks out
at the long grass thinking she should cut it

when the green thickens in one part and moves
revealing a woodpecker that probes and tugs.

In all that grass the head stands forward, crimson.
For a moment she leaves herself at the window

and enters the green sphere where light is carried
under birds' wings and between their feathers

to snowdrops and bird-lime splashed on the grass.
Now the woodpecker has flown into a quince tree,

where it sits upright on a branch and preens the down
on its moss-green breast, the red cap

bobbing about in the twigs' gold frame.
She carries that light back with her, carefully.

## GLOSE: WATER AND STONE

*'I am a woman sixty years old and of no special courage.*
*Everyday – a little conversation with God, or his envoy the*
*tall pine, or the grass-swimming cricket.*
*Everyday – I study the difference between water and stone.*
*Everyday – I stare at the world; I push the grass aside*
*and stare at the world.'*

*Mary Oliver, 'Work'.*

As I drive over a body of land on a ribbon
of tarmac west from Fishguard there's a wolf's castle
of rocks against a sky so wide, so unbroken
that I think for an instant of what I bring, scars
where a breast lived, neck held with a pin, seven
(at least) of my nine lives gone. But this damage
may mend – and light in high places is vast
and unfolds, nameless, like something given.
Most like a sexual pang, a silent pledge:
I am a woman sixty years old and of no special courage.

Stacked in uneven layers, accretions of heat
shimmer above a field and corral horses
in a small group under sheltering alder trees
too far away to see, but I imagine water,
leaves mouthing over a muddy stream,
breeze and breath – God doesn't come into it –
the horses stock still, while straw-coloured stalks
of cow-parsley sway under spread loads of seeds,
packed seed-heads whispering their dry secrets
to the tall pine or the grass-swimming cricket.

Motionless, the estuary today, brim-full
and monochrome; each grass-blade mirrors
itself in perfect symmetry, each white gull
floats on its own double. Even the kingfishers
are paired – in air, not water – flying parallel
to the path, two black specks until they turn
under the bridge and there's a flash of blue brighter
than toffee-paper, a miracle as small and usual
as stone breaking water, water polishing stone.
Everyday I study the difference between water and stone.

I'd like to think that part of what I see
when I gaze at the world – those stopped moments
when the breath is knocked away – might be
imprinted on my chromosomes. Then, once
my ninth and last life fails, the cells finally
close and all the atoms disperse, I'll meld
with specks of stone and grass, become fragments
in the dust particulate spinning daily
from dark to light to dark. Sixty years old:
I push the grass aside and stare at the world.

## NEWFOUNDLAND

Through the big glass doors to the balcony
I see it's starting to snow in slow motion.
Birds emerge through the snow-curtain:

a flicker pulling long black seeds
from the feeder, juncos jumping, but chickadees
won't come until the flicker takes flight.

'Chickadee' – that's what our mother called us
when we were small; later, a word I found
for my daughter. Now, continents divide us

but for today we're sitting together quietly,
just my sister and I in her woodstove-warmed room
watching it snow. Birds, I'm never far from –

give them half a chance and they fly in –
and something in the way the flakes float down
with the dark shapes of birds pressing through them

brings Ben to mind, our cousin who's lived on the streets
for years and thinks he's got his work cut out
keeping all the coloured balls and little sticks

in the air at once, that no less is expected of him,
and whose mother lies awake these snowy nights
praying that he's alive, has a doorway to sleep in.

## AT THE PARTY

We're in an old waterworks building,
the high room like a large empty tank
filled with the memory of water,

windows at the far end flooding us
with light from the grey outside. In here
there's more gleam, and shadowy ripples

lap round the jazz saxophonist's feet.
And because of the music, because
of what it fills you with, this poem

should be for you – small girl, young woman,
I don't know which – just as I don't know
your name, only that you're the daughter

of my friend's friend, that you might be twelve
or thirteen, that you have Down's and that
if this party will bring me sadness

before it ends, it will also give
me a present you don't know is yours
to bestow, something I've tucked away

in a spare synapse like an old tune.
While we're having dinner I spot you
way across the room, yours the brightest,

most eager face, eating with gusto,
talking to everyone, all non-stop.
And when the evening dims and the sky

goes deep, you're whirled out on to the floor
by an older man who's placed one hand
carefully in the small of your back

to hold you steady, and now you're off,
sliding a bit at first then, bolder,
twirling round under his outstretched arm

until you're dizzy and out of breath
and flop on a chair. Here the floor-show
really begins: while the saxophone

plays softly the man passes his hands
behind you – you're embarrassed, laughing –
and – snap! – lo and behold! – produces

small red lights from the back of your neck,
origami flowers from your sleeve.
You're so brimming with delight it spills

over us; as for me, I'm in it
up to the eyes. And what my friend says
to me before we go, what she fears

and knows is lodged in her body, that,
too, I'm secreting somewhere about
my person, pushing it up my sleeve.

## OPUS 20

Eight young players, the composer
  only sixteen when he wrote his Octet,
and us in our sixties, waiting, friends
  for two lifetimes. When you say
'life-threatening' it gives me a jolt…
  but we don't speak of tomorrow,
not until we say goodbye.
  And as Mendelssohn begins

a gate opens in me – in you
  too, I think, for music to enter.
It rushes in *con fuoco*; under
  faded mosaics in the dome
the strands of sound fan out
  and close, each urgent question
passing round the semi-circle
  from one player to the next.

The brilliance is within. It fills
  our thirsty hollows, wakes in us
the freshness of first things,
  a wildness, the world ahead.
Dear friend, lick your finger
  and place it on this thread
next to mine; we'll follow it
  together, wherever it goes.

## RITORNELLO

Umber sand, ridged,
  green weed-strands flung on it.

A rock makes an island halfway to the water,
  its barnacles dry and dusty;

in the pool at the rock's foot
  an almost transparent fish

slips its long backbone freely
  from shallow to dark.

A couple picking mussels, the sea
  a faraway roar. Nothing else.

Another world
  where everything's scrubbed and scoured,

gleaming like tin.
  What childhood should have been.

## FOR V.H.

Every full moon this year huge clouds have rolled
across the sky like weightless breakers poised
to fall. These were your dark nights. In February
I looked across the field towards your house
to see if your light was on, relieved that it wasn't.
But when we met for the last time and you blessed me –
you so hollow, so bent – and asked for my prayers,
I found no words to give you, no, not one.

Yet I couldn't have wished more strongly to keep you
from suffering. When the blanks between the stars went chalky
in the brightness, you seemed part of the immensity,
of whatever in space is stretching away towards
a horizon where all borderlines are blurred,
one among many with stars, creatures, children.

## WILD LIFE

the poster promises, rooted in the broken arches
of the Ponte Rotto, but all we can see from the new bridge
is straggly bushes blowing in the wind.

Disappointed, we look down the embanked ravine
to where the Cloaca Maxima, the Great Drain
discharges into the Tiber, and there on top

on the flat masonry blocks is a building-site hut,
a frame hung with bits of cloth and tarpaulins
so well protected you'd only spot it by chance,

and then I see that some of the cloths are clothes
and the long black stripes are socks hanging to dry,
draped over the side. It's a camp, a castle;

somebody's made his home in this dry vault
high above the river. But how does he live?
We hurry down the steps to the disused tow-path

and here he's visible, but so far up on his arch
he's hard to see, a small figure eating
and putting food on little trays for the cats.

And, although we're home again, he grows in my mind;
I remember a cold Spring, petals and snowflakes
floating down together, almond and plum

with scarcely more colour than snow, how calm that made me,
and I think that's what he wants, above the drain,
the ebb and flow of the river, the water's motion,

to feel the pull of the sea at night on the lonely
tow-path and walk to the pulse of wind and rain,
slowing his mind to their relentless measure.

## THE END OF TIME

On this bitter January night
sometime after six o'clock, with snow
blowing under the barrack door

in Stalag VIIIA, rows of prisoners,
skeletons hung with rags
against the Silesian winter,

listen – for an hour, for their lives –
to what no-one has ever heard before.
What hunger for it in the men listening,

the blue-orange chords on the keyboard
falling weightless, the colours of sunrise,
and each new cadence sounding like home.

How many gathered there – five hundred,
five thousand? No-one remembers.
Whatever the number, all still

as if an angel crowned with a rainbow
had come and sounded the trumpet
as a sign that time has ended.

Wearing clogs, playing a broken piano
the composer asks the impossible:
the clarinettist must hold his note

until he leaves earth behind, the cellist
move his bow so inhumanly slowly
he reaches towards silence.

They feel their way through pathless rhythms.
'Never', Messiaen says, 'have I been listened to
with such attention, such understanding.'

## AT LAUGHARNE

In the pause before the ebb, the sea
  balanced between coming and going,
a small hut – maybe for tools
  or fishing-gear – stands perfect
in its plainness among tussocks of salt-marsh,
  perfectly reflected in water
so that where I'm standing is the one point
  where two worlds are visible,
the small grey hut and its double –
  then the retreat, reflux,
a slipping away as the estuary opens
  like a hand, re-mapping sandbanks,
mudflats and all the channels
  between them in a gathering of light and air.

Did you look down at this body of land and sea
  unconfined in skin, feel your veins
and arteries branching and subject
  to the same flow and pull as the waters?
When you escaped from cramped indoors
  it was to the four walls
of your writing-hut high on the cliff,
  its floor covered with discarded drafts,
beer bottles on the desk,
  all the frowsty mess of life and poetry
until the hour when you slid out on a breath
  into the bay and were immersed
in the expanse: you, Dylan, in your loaded ark
  setting forth on the flood.

## READING TRAHERNE

*Eternity is a sphere*
*into which we enter*

*all whose parts are at once*
*standing round about us*

but for me it's more like water –
depth rather than surface

slightly salted, thin, a bit clouded,
rich with nutrients –

and navigating through the dark
with other swimming creatures,

shoals of mackerel, shadowy whales,
their blips of radar,

the line swinging round a dial
in a green continuum.

## VISITANTS

Suddenly, across the hot shimmer of ferns,
horses, thirty or forty of them
massed against a backdrop of sea and sky,

bright-coloured, waiting, expectant,
as if they'd been there from the start,
somewhere we could only half recall:

why had they picked their way along
this winding path, stepping with delicate hooves
between heather and the coiled roots of blueberry

right to the peak, small heaps of dried dung
marking their route, and stood,
face-on to the wind, looking out?

Nothing to graze on; just rock this close
to the edge, and a few flowers – scabious,
campion, tormentil lodged in the cracks.

They must have gazed into a space
so blank, so unfocused in its melding
of blue-green and blue,

it was as if they were inside it,
part of the light that pulled the sea's thread,
of an expanse we could only long for.

In their stillness they seemed
like pictures from a child's story-book,
larger than life, fabulous.

To them we were no more than rocks
or trees to brush past, neutral,
but they made me afraid;

I couldn't walk among them,
push past their warm flanks,
feel their breathing, the deep-veined necks.

As they move on together,
mares and foals pressed close, they seem
to carry with them a kind of darkness

as if we'd looked too near the sun –
small plants, birds, stones, all alive in the dark –
and I thought of the mares giving birth,

how their tissues would soften and dilate
so the young could be pushed into the light,
and how close unfold is to enfold.

## SOUNDINGS

When the sensor moved across her skin
she saw the baby hold his hands over his face

as if he were distressed. Two inches long,
his back towards us, head, body, limbs

and beating heart: how sharp it is,
this fuzzy image. He has no words, no hopes

or thought, only instinct and shallow memories
like those that bewilder an animal.

And passages can open out of time:
I wake one day in the dark hearing birdsong, step

from the house to the earthy smell of Spring
and plunge in, long spine, breath easy,

like swimming with free strokes, balanced and held,
with all the blackbirds that ever were, singing.

## AS DEW

*He cam also stille*
*There his moder was,*
*As dew in Aprille*
*That falleth on the grass.*

Inky seas that could be mackerel
feeding in shoals just below
the surface, light catching them
as they turn sharp faces to the horizon,
a shimmering oil-skim on ripples:

hour by hour, stars pass my window,
the Milky Way's soft diagonal, Orion
on wobbly legs, the Small Triangle,
until towards morning, sky deepens
and matches the blue of parted curtains.

Frost, I see, has come to the grass, a powdery
blue ghost, more unearthly than silver,
without bending the slightest blade.

## LIFE STORY

Night, and you step out into blackness, over
the side of the silent vessel, dreading that you
or your boots might slip and miss the rung, one
false move your last. Between above and below
you hang breathless, locked into history –
and this is what you chose, what you want.

No moon, no stars – though light's not what you want –
only a sound like a thumb rubbing over
corrugated card as the men in your story
run down the ladder, loaded with kit. And you
feel rather than see, where the man below
you wavers, shifts his pack, now there's no-one.

'Dropped like a stone,' I hear you say, 'just one
splash and he'd gone.' A small smile. You want
to cry, can't quite believe the man below
the water wasn't you, rehearse it over
and over again to convince yourself that you
survived the war, came home to tell your story.

It comes back to me now: hearing your story
I saw what you saw, clear as glass, how someone
plummeted down, but whether it was you,
or him, or someone else, I didn't want
to know. Slid through a door that closed over
his head, from dark above to dark below.

Whoever that man was who plunged below,
if you're the secret sharer of his story
then I'm yours. And the story isn't over;
when you dropped like a stone you left me one
part short, however much I wanted – want –
to understand the plot and why I miss you.

Taller than life, younger than in death, you
come to visit me now from way below
the spirit-level of dream; won't speak. I want
to ask if you can love me – that old story –
but don't; put my arms around you one
last time and say, I love you, over and over.

I conjured you from below by telling your story
and then I saw our two stories are one:
can I want yours to end before mine's over?

## COW PARSLEY

There's a kind of silence like the quiet
of a listening-booth,

somewhere to stay for a while,
an empty cathedral, say,

in the presence of something unknown
and become permeable to,

tinged with colour, cloud,
whatever is indubitably here

and insistent as the Cow Parsley
just come into bloom,

(how lightly the stalk bends
as a bird lands

how quickly it springs back
when the tiny weight lifts)

here, too,
in the spaces between its florets,

in the fretted shadows
under all umbelliferous flowers.

## BY FAVERSHAM CREEK

Transfixed by a bush, the hips so brilliant,
so complete in their redness I'm taken
to a place where nothing's missing –

though people are – and the thought
of my sister who's ill and so far away
is the shadow of this, the under-drawing.

Nothing for me to do but walk –
past a toad, motionless
under a cover of weeds,

by the side of dried-out ditches
choked with milkweed and teasel
towards a field-gate. Beyond it

a wild rose-bush suddenly opens
and blossoms with birds, goldfinches
packed close on every twig

dazzling even amongst rose-hips
as they extend yellow wings to preen,
bowing their scarlet heads.

## MEWSLADE BAY

*for Flora*

Today the wind's blowing off the shore,
ramming the damp sand hard down the beach
into the sea spray

where the four of us, random figures
in a landscape, are brought together
at Mewslade by you,

your birthday thirty years ago, all
the usual accidents of time and
place, now, in this wind.

'I'd stay all day, if there were shelter,'
I tell you, but there's not, so we drift
back towards rock pools

and watch small sea-anemones, wine-
red, clamped fast to the smooth walls, clinging
on for life itself.

Leaning in, we touch these hemispheres
of lustrous jelly, softly wrinkle
skin that's cool and sweet,

seeing how underwater they turn
into flowers and wave their petal-
tentacles, guileless.

Sometimes it helps to take the long view:
to feel our lives, our frailties, held in
a moment of sand

and stinging cold, a salt clarity
of water, the bunches of red dulse
swinging their thin leaves

in slow ripples under our hands, and
all around, the imperceptible
movement of limestone.

## HIRAETH

Because I ask about ‘hiraeth’ you send me
Waldo Williams’ poem which yearns to number
the nameless dead, remember the forgotten –

and the poem’s in my mind as we open
the door to find a thrush on the steps, dying.
She’s breathing fast; her splashed breast heaves as the heart

struggles on. There’s no blood, no visible wound.
For a moment we freeze – then you scoop her up
into your palm, cup the other hand over

and place her in the shade of a broad-leaved bush.
When I next look, the bird is dead. And dead, seems
only half the size, so bedraggled is she,

so flattened and dusty. Her eyes are closed now,
her head turned to one side as if at the end
she looked inward, longing to see beyond life,

to accept the dark that will come, pitiful
in her materiality – as we are
in yearning that a single spark might survive.

*hiraeth* is the Welsh word for a range of emotions
including longing, yearning, homesickness, and occurs
in Waldo Williams’ poem ‘*Cofio*’, ‘Remembering’.

## FREE FALL

On the edge, scarcely caught
    by gravity's pull,
an astronaut
        or topsy-turvy deep
        sea diver, balanced to keep
giddy ledge-perched feet, hands, eyes steady

in the face of so much
    blue, I pierce air, drop
sight-lines to touch
        rock, shoal, submarine cliff
        close-up, all as clear as if
immaterial. A blotched boulder's

lapped by lazy wave-slaps
    in transparent green
surge and relapse
        and is suddenly thrust
        clean out of the water, just
like a man in a sleek bronze helmet

in lift-off to the sun.
    What kind of merman
is this? Not one
        to trust as he slips on
        a glossy fur pelt, flips on
his back, gazes at me and smiles with

seal-brown, beckoning eyes
    as if expecting
I'd recognise
        and greet him. And it's true,
        some place I know him, in blue
floodlit depths where wave folds over wave

and we slowly rotate,
    selkie skin to skin,
suspended weight-
        less as I smooth his slick
        nape, listen to the rhythmic
long-drawn breaths, my head against his chest.

## FLYCATCHER

Thinking about birds, all those lives
parallel to ours, and a word

alights, too heavy
for their slight bodies

unburdened as they are;
what they build is easy

as breath, weightless as the cloud-
shaped cup under leaves

a flycatcher has pieced
together with twigs, threads

and a ragged length of wool
that waves like a banner.

Twice I walk past;
each time she takes me lightly

into her eyes, returns my gaze
so brightly, so creature to creature –

this brown-as-a-mouse bird –
that my soul is shaken

open, expands and takes wing
with only that weighty word to steady it –

*tenderness*; yes,
tender, as a bruise is.

# SONNETS FOR A CHILD

Only a chance encounter on a train;
her mother parks the push-chair by my seat
and the baby's eyes meet mine. Hers are violet-
blue and her eyelashes long and curly. When
I look away she calls and crows again,
claims my attention. Her hair's a little wet;
they've come from a swimming class, Esmé quiet
and fearless held in her mother's arms, even
underwater.
                    Now it's my station stop;
I wait while the train pulls away to see
if Esmé's waving – absurd! – then walk back up
the platform slowly, almost overwhelmed
by a sense of longing, of never-having-had,
those years of my child's childhood lost to me.

Those years of my child's childhood lost to me
re-make themselves in dream. I'm underwater,
pushing with strong feet as I clasp my daughter's
small form tucked in against my breasts and we
surge through deepest blue creating streams
of bubbles round our legs, so close that whether
she's holding on to me or I'm claiming her
no-one could tell. But in reality
why did I lose those years, where did they go?
Nobody was to blame; my back gave way –
torn ligaments, slipped discs – and bed-bound, home-bound,
never able to lift her from that day,
I had to give her up to other hands,
bite back my tears and wait for her to grow.

To cope with loss and wait for her to grow,
however hard, was the only choice I had
but that excision left a space, a void
nothing can altogether fill. Below
conscious thought, there must be a shadow
memory in most of us of being carried
firmly in someone's familiar arms, sheltered
against the chest and hearing the heart's hollow
thud.

So mothers in Raphael's drawing run
holding their babes, vainly trying to fend
off blows with their bodies; so in Iraq, a child,
innocent scrap, sick with pneumonia, was held
round-eyed and trusting, in Margaret Hassan's
hands; so, in our turn, we'd wish to hold.

Hands that in our turn we want to hold –
mother first, then child – hands that caress
or are unkind, slap or stroke a face,
link us, through their touch, with a wider world.
In my case, of course, I wished to hold
on to the child I loved; the empty space
foreshadowed a later loss, the loneliness
of letting go when she'd grown. She's older
now than I was when she was born but that
instinct lives on, to gather a child to the breast,
to smooth her hair – like silk, or damp with rain –
and connects me in that simple human gesture
with other lives, whether near or far apart,
or glimpsed in a chance encounter on a train.

## THE ROAD

Think ‘Silk Road’ and you might think
        of apricots in Kashgar,
                spices and perfumes packaged

in paper-lined boxes, jade
        and lapis, dumb beasts laden
                with rugs and bolts of satin.

What you might not imagine
        is a hundred and fifty
                camels at a water-hole,

their polyphonic music
        way below the lowest line
                on the bass stave, single strands

of grief sung to emptiness
        and desiccation knotted
                into the one sad fabric.

Dry sand embalms; what it hides
        is immune to time and change:
                small stained shoes, lost love letters,

a child’s embroidered jacket,
        desert rats, camels, stray dogs
                and humped skeletons of men.

## THE CLEARING

We'd walked a new way in the woods, down
to the next valley then back to where
someone had carved out a meadow after the war

so that coming at it afresh was like a vision
of somewhere unknown, somewhere green
and gold, with the fennel in flower

and the air humming. I half expected
to see cherubs clustered overhead
like swallows with crossed tail-feathers

while we waited the arrival of the angel
and the message. Back home, a wasp
clings to a leaf, sunlight to a wall;

surely these can bear the weight
of meditation, common things
opening in the mind like a fan painted

with clouds and plum-blossom
and two lovers who've paused halfway across
a half-moon bridge? At night, awake

and listening to a rhythmic patter like footfalls,
I know it's been a good season for owls,
the tawny ones that call and call,

their songs descending in steps to spiral
the house while all else is silent;
by the time their wordless cries

echo inside me, I'm running so lightly
down their rich staircase that I fall and sleep.
But underneath all this there's something else

that won't go away, an abstract and nameless
anguish that needs to hear those soft owl-voices
singing clear in the dark from the far side

of a field or a wood. O life, how we cling to it!
In cold tones, love reconfigures:
each day I wonder what will change for ever.

## LOVE SONG

The air spicy, appetising,
sheen on the mud,
barges with dark-red sails

moving towards the creek,
you by my side. (And will
you read this ever, feel pleased or sad?)

A spell that can't be broken,
not even by the wet spaniel
who cocks his leg against the bench

as each moment sings 'perfection'
and being perfect
is also filled with longing.

## THE BUOY

I couldn't make it out at first:
a green triangle, strangely visible
and floating on nothing

but there was so much more to watch
from the marsh on a winter afternoon
that I forgot that shape, what with a flock

of black-tailed godwits on the foreshore
driving their long beaks down to retrieve
delicacies I could only guess at

from the sand's soft store-room, teal
flying their yellow pennants on pools
behind the high sea-wall, and wigeon

gaudy in plum and tawny. And when curlew
rose and flew down the length of the estuary,
I knew there was something specially attuned

to their music in our innermost ear
and not only to their cries, but to
oyster-catcher and avocet, stonechat and coot

and that this was the most unalloyed
happiness I could have, to be here
in their midst, with the green light

of the buoy shining out
and seeing the subtle waters recede,
the gradual revelation of mud-shine.

## DUNGENESS

There's almost nothing between the sky
          and the shingle but colour
                    that falls in strings of beads

from clouds holding on to their rain.
          Ground level, and sea-cabbages unpack
                    their limp leaves;

terns and black-backed gulls sit further off
          in a row, all facing one way,
                    sideways to the sun.

It's not that something's about to start
          nor that anything's happened;
                    no-one's around,

it's just slumped red-brown blackberries, dunlin
          clustered overhead, and a small plane
                    disappearing towards Lydd.

## LAUNDRY

Low tide, high wind; sailboarders and clouds
slip across horizontals, slice air
to bright untied ribbons which stream out
behind a girl with unplaited hair

who's running by the edge of the sea
where colour threads through light, like satin
ruffling a frill at neckline or sleeve,

and bunched wavetips of creamy linen
fall crumpled on shore. When I think *fresh*
it smells like this, the water as green
as a bar of Sunlight soap, washing

me back to a small house, a Monday,
you and me alone in the kitchen
in the half-sweet, damp scent of laundry.

On the gas stove there's a fizzy brew
of whites in a large tub. You poke them
with a dolly stick, add Reckitt's Blue
in its little bag through clouds of steam

then plunge blindly through the thick lather
with long wooden tongs, spattering foam.
Rinsing is an up and down matter,

red fists jumping and diving like fish
in swirls of bleached slow-motion sea-weed.
You dry your fingers gently; I wish
they weren't so cracked and sore, their creases

split apart. You let me help glue them
together with Nu-skin; your hands feel
rough as the kitchen towel, and as warm.

All this air's gone to my head; leaning
into the salt gale I watch the sea
ruffle its green, and it's like looking
straight down into that small room, as real

and clear as a bar of soap that's caught
the light. We still sit there, drinking tea,
you with a Woodbine, and talk and talk;

we never dry up. I see you comb
my hair into scrawny plaits, then find
freshly ironed blue ribbons to tie them:
two figures, spotlit by a window,

bright as glass. But although I'm listening,
what with the boom of water and wind,
I can't hear a word you're saying.

## ACCOMMODATION

Imagine this: your father dies.
You bury him under your house, in a hastily
scrabbled place among dirt and stones
and share his silence, his wasting away.
Then your first duty: to take his crumbs
in your mouth, drink the broth of his bones.

Yes, father, that's Ancient China,
but haven't you been buried under my floorboards
all this time? It's twenty years
since you died; a long discarnation.
Now in my sleep I know you're there,
huddled in the black earth.

It was your hand stretched out to me
in dream; I know how the blue wrist-veins
run distinct under the blue-white skin.
I couldn't take it in mine – as I couldn't
hold your pipe, your specs when you'd died –
threw them – forgive me – straight in the bin.

There were men with your hands on the pier
at Deal, fishing under a purple sky,
deliberate fingers stiff against weights
and tackle, threading worms on hooks.
They had your look, facing out
on emptiness, quietly waiting.

I could have watched them for hours. The sea
was all opaque jade surface
and I thought of cod, the way gold
is splashed on their flanks, how
they make heavy headway through the traffic
of tide and current, in the Atlantic cold.

I'm homing in on you now, father,
picking my way through debris, deposits
from our old life, each packed layer,
till I can swallow this thing that is you
in a sort of makeshift accommodation
impossible while we shared air.

## JURY

I'd noticed her hands before, large and quiet
in her lap as she listened through all the words
for the sound she wanted, the call from her scrap
of daughter, fed on demand
while we waited

and I thought of how she'd hold that feather-weight
in one hand while the other cupped the warm head
with its beating fontanelle close to her breast
as if that soft suck and tug
were all the world

and she could forget the knife, (one of a set),
with the serrated edge we'd seen already,
an ordinary kitchen knife, its ten-inch blade
nestling securely inside
a cling-wrapped box.

But it was the photo made me cry – her hand,
in colour, the palm flat for the camera,
fingers stretched apart to show the base of each
cut to the bone, ragged wounds
only half healed:

how painful it must have been to open out
the sheltering fist, uncurl her fingers and feel
the tight scabs crack, exposed for an indifferent
photographer to record
the naked truth.

And the moment all the others led up to
and away from – the moment before her hand
lost its grip on a handle made slippery with
his blood, slid down the blade? – that,
we couldn't see.

## THE FALL

Was it foreshadowed,
that plunge down a dark stairwell,
when I wrote only hours beforehand

of golden berries at dusk
hanging their heads, the rich clusters
in a darker brilliance

taking me to the edge,
so that one small step further
would break the surface?

When I walked out into blackness,
felt the void under my foot
and arrived where that took me

all my moments scattered,
separate, on a blank
shadowless field.

## WHAT YOU CALLED ME

'Lazarus,' you say smiling.
And for an instant the same image
hovers unmentioned
in the air between us –

a pale figure stepping forward
eagerly into the light,
almost as white as the cloth he drops
to the ground and still
with the taint of death on him.

## GRACE

Through the window too many greens,
  dense, hang motionless, overblown
with lush; all that isn't leaf is lacy,

  the patches of sky with crinkled edges
and a net of song-lines two blackbirds
  are throwing backwards and forwards

in complicated call and response.
  Rain-spots fall singly patterning
a roof-cloth, then faster and faster,

  fresh, orchestral, until rallentando
fades to random. Seems random.
  But as each large drop strikes,

a leaf resonates, thrums, and the tree
  becomes its own music-master,
rain-maker, creates what it devours,

  an outpouring that falls from invisible
heights grain by grain, greening
  almost before it touches the ground.

## RIO DARRO

Down through the clear air of the high sierras,
down wooded slopes, round Alhambra's hill
the Darro gathers snow-melt in its channel
and flings its icy gold-bearing waters

to the edge of the city until it disappears
through what Lorca calls an 'absurd' tunnel
and the cold music is lost under the marble-
paved streets, the bars and fake flamenco *zambras*,

under, too, some shabby tenement
where a gypsy singer visited by darkness
sobs out his soul's pain in the bitter accent

of *cante hondo*, deep song of the oppressed,
relentless as the flow of a hidden torrent
now and then breaking through to the surface.

## IN GRANADA

Outside it's daytime,
the sky purple and violet,
the greens too bright

but we turn aside
into a church,
the brown grainy emptiness

where rain's rhythm
is so loud on the roof
it leaves no room for thought

and two recorders, invisible,
rise above the rain
and take it into their music.

*

Lorca, I want to walk
round the back of one of your poems
and sit in its shade
while light drops on the pavement
through the pierced windows
of your words.

*

Now a child is standing in front
of the full-length looking-glass
in her wardrobe door
saying *I am me, I am me*
until it seems she is
and *I* steps into *me*
with all the little left-over bits
glinting in the mirror's
bevelled edges.

## EASTER CANDLES

i.

Caught off guard – these moments
always coming obliquely, just a glance
over her shoulder at a child
and a mother carrying the weight

of a foetus lightly – she imagines
what swims inside a womb,
the curled shape, little fish, starfish,
sea-anemone with frondy fingers

and it breaks over her, from her,
what she can't have again, never
to nuzzle against small hair-smell,
lips brushing the beating membrane

as she remembers holding a baby
pressed to her chest,
the gravity-pull of it, warm
head centred between her breasts.

ii.

Daffodils and sweet-peas standing
in water, before the knowledge of them,
just as they're coming into being,
and she looks through the glass, the water,

to the bubbles in the water, how they pearl
the side of the glass, rise and burst,
like something swimming, little sea-horse
bobbing about in warm salty fluid,

a line of bubbles rising to the surface
and that was it, that's what she'd felt,
the first touch, the certainty, uncurling
through millions of years to its new creation.

iii.

How the body shines through:
a light behind tissue paper, the fine
clinging of cloth to skin, small flesh
embedded in a larger space,

she thinks of it pushing its heels hard
on the wall, the throb of almost transparent
limbs though this time the cry's a cry
of pain as she heaves a great weight

through narrowness, her one desire
now to bring it to light, deliver
herself from this urgent longing,
and it breaks through, surfaces

headfirst like a swimmer, bluefish, wet,
the skin filmed with wax, and dazed,
frowning until breath fills the mouth
and nostrils, a baby cries herself pink.

iv.

A cloud shifts and as if just surfaced,
innocent, the small dusty park
fills with green, expands
in the wet light, each drop a world

glistening in close-up, words
she wants to hold on to, as she knows
she won't see that particular freshness
again, and later, driving home,

thinking – the candles are finished
for this year, the white Easter candles
on the horse chestnut, the flame gone,
just the grainy seeds and the dark tree –

the sudden glimpse of it, the burst,
the sheer sideways swipe of it –
*how beauty hurts* – knocks her flying,
because what can she do with it?

## ON OARE MARSHES

A cold afternoon, the tide
  rolled back, redshanks stabbing
at ooze on the foreshore
  when a child lifts her head
and says, 'Don't you remember,

  fifty years ago you climbed
right to the top of Golden Cap
  and stopped, breathless,
seeing for the first time how
  green the sky is, how wide the water?'

## DESIRE

Such a presence, glimpsed unexpectedly
from the window, and so luminous
my heart jumps: it could be the bird,

the very same woodpecker,
stepped out of the poem I'd imagined
it into, the one who came to my friend

the afternoon her husband died,
carrying her into its realm
of varied light and, like this bird

looming brilliant over the lawn,
neither avatar nor apparition
but warm-blooded as I am

while at the back of it all
another bird drums out
Morse code, double quick,

and there's so much to attend to –
all those voices – that I think
if we could decipher even a part

our flesh and bones might become
transparent and our skin
glow gold, like a Buddha's.

Such desire! – and it's not that we long
for flowers and birds *more* than people,
but they're so close, so small

and tender, unfearful of death
or heartache, that they can't help
but awaken love easily.

## LORDS AND LADIES

*'All promises are fleshed*
*or now they fail.'*

*Charles Tomlinson, 'October'.*

Although this pair are making towards wilt-down
they're still all sap and go
in the late summer scuff of the hedge,

two naked stems springing
from dusty twigs and dry jumble,
the few berries on each tip

in orange clusters, their skins tight
to bursting, inviting and shiny
as if they'd been varnished.

On this dark August day their fruit
are bright pomegranates
packed with seeds, seed-pearls,

pearly eggs, and I remember promises
fleshed and failed, and how hard it is
to feel the freshness of things

but Lords and Ladies know nothing of that;
their torchlight draws small animals
who snuff up ripeness in globules

and carry the seeds safe in their warm gut
before leaving them, uncovered,
to fend for themselves.

## WHITE CYCLAMEN

I've read that in Japanese
there's a word – *yugen* – for 'flower'
that doesn't mean 'blossom' but is an unseen
ghost-flower, breathless, timeless.

Think of white cyclamen
on a window-sill – how they gain
an extra whiteness from the reflected
shine of snow outside

so that although in time their petals
one by one will twist and fade
they still retain a grey shadow, an under-self
more beautiful than brightness –

and it's hard not to think that flowers have souls
if soul is the breathless, timeless part of us.

## TOWARDS THE DEEP NORTH

Traveller of the narrow road, with your regular
satchel pulling on your collar-bone

and rucking up your threadbare coat of blue-grey and blue,
burdened by nothing of much value

but the long musings in your mind's deep pond, where a stone
may drop or a frog jump or the moon

drift on the still surface; content never to arrive
more than halfway there, nor, much, to grieve

for those friends who waved you goodbye: oh, lonely story-
teller, truth-seeker, I love you more

as I get older – and wait for a thought to balance –
was I, too, your road companion once?

## MORANDI'S JUGS

As if you turned away
from your carnivorous city,
fat, red Bologna,

its salami pink brick,
all the crimsons, terracottas,
the blotched purple marble

and scraped down your palette
to see how things look
when nobody's looking.

Your bloodless vases and jugs
are pure vegetarian;
when the small fluted bowl blushes

it's tipped in faintest lilac.
They huddle together, backs
towards us, avoid our eyes;

there's tenderness in the air.
I think I've fallen in love
with the shy white teapot.

## BLUE TITS

No need to look for colour,
it searches me out, crimson

and white anemones
fixing my eye as I read

the fine cursive on the underside
of cupped flower-heads

wanting them to last and last
in a greed for eternity

so that even the slightest crumple
on a white petal touches me –

and I cram it all in, wondering
how I could live without colour

feathering the air, afraid
of blue and brightness, of losing

sight of the material world
as I stare into the garden and follow

small birds along invisible tracks
inside the bay tree

until they conjure themselves
out of the leaves,

their eyes excited
by wavelengths of green light.

## GANNET

This is what I came to look for
          from the rocks at the very tip
                    of St David's Head, this bird,

this gannet, so white it reflects the light
          from far out on the open sea,
                    one continuous line of body

aimed towards
          the questing head and sharp beak,
                    its whole being flowing forward

like Braque's bird, bleached
          and flying over the bay,
                    back to Grassholm.

Suppose I could be re-born
          into that frame, what might I find
                    in the huge plunge seaward,

the crash of entry, the long
          descent to semi-darkness?
                    What fish emerge with?